FOR

I THINK YOU'D ENJOY THIS BOOK BECAUSE

FROM

PRINCIPLES FOR THE NEXT CENTURY OF WORK

Sense & Respond Press publishes short, beautiful, actionable books on topics related to innovation, digital transformation, product management, and design. Our readers are smart, busy, practical innovators. Our authors are experts working in the fields they write about.

The goal of every book in our series is to solve a real-world problem for our readers. Whether that be understanding a complex and emerging topic, or something as concrete (and difficult) as hiring innovation leaders, our books help working professionals get better at their jobs, quickly.

Jeff Gothelf & Josh Seiden

Series co-editors **Jeff Gothelf** and **Josh Seiden** wrote *Lean UX* (O'Reilly) and *Sense & Respond* (Harvard Business Review Press) together. They were co-founding Principals of Neo Innovation (sold to Pivotal Labs) in New York City and helped build it into one of the most recognized brands in modern product strategy, development, and design. In 2017 they were short-listed for the Thinkers50 award for their contributions to innovation leadership. Learn more about Jeff and Josh at www.jeffgothelf.com and www.joshseiden.com.

Lateral Leadership
A practical guide for Agile Product Managers
Tim Herbig

The Invisible Leader
Facilitation secrets for catalyzing change,
cultivating innovation, and commanding results
Elena Astilleros

The Government Fix
How to innovate in government
Hana Schank & Sara Hudson

Outcomes Over Output
Why customer behavior is the key metric for business success
Josh Seiden

To keep up with new releases or submit book ideas to the press
check out our website at www.senseandrespondpress.com

WHAT CEOs NEED TO KNOW ABOUT DESIGN

Issued in print and electronic formats.

ISBN 978-1-7036350-5-8 (KDP paperback)

Editor: Victoria Olsen
Designer: Mimi O Chun
Interior typesetting: Jennifer Blais

Published in the United States by Sense & Respond Press
www.senseandrespondpress.com

Printed and bound in the United States.

1 2 3 4   22 21 20 19

Audrey Crane

WHAT CEOs NEED TO KNOW ABOUT DESIGN
KNOW ABOUT DESIGN

A business leader's guide to
working with designers

SENSE &
RESPOND
PRESS

INTRODUCTION

A few months ago, the CEO of a 200-person, $25M B2B (business-to-business) company called me. He said, "As a former developer, I understand technology. I've learned about running my company's finances, HR, Marketing, and Operations. I believe design is crucial for my company's success. But I don't know about design, and I don't know *how* to know. Can you help me?"

What a question! Where to start?

Also, why hadn't more executives asked me this? Design has been the "new black" for 10 years! At least 50 VC and analyst reports tout the value of design. That's why every new company wants to be the "Apple of" something.

I started interviewing Business Leaders who were not Designers themselves, but who had seen success after advocating for design in their organizations. I asked how they became advocates, why they believed in design, and what value it provided. That was how I discovered some wide gaps in their knowledge and expectations. This aligned with what I've learned from 20 years of helping clients design software, run design teams, and uncover opportunities for meaningful innovation; and supporting the design process necessary to realize their ideas. These lessons provided the foundation for this book.

WHY IT MATTERS

Design is happening in your organization—and not just in marketing or advertising, but whenever anyone builds a mobile app, web site, or digital product. The alternative to good design isn't no design; it's bad design. When product managers make wireframes, they're doing design. When Engineers add a front-end so they can see functionality, they're doing design. When Marketing asks the Engineers to add a logo and the "right" colors, they're doing design.

The important questions are:
» Are you intentional in crafting your customers' experiences?
» How closely do customer experiences map to your intent?
» And overall, is design helping or hindering your organization?

Just as your product and customers will struggle if your Engineers' code is deeply flawed, your product and customers will struggle if the user experience is deeply flawed.

Some companies have succeeded despite fragile or poorly designed software. However, there are innumerable companies in the dead pool precisely because of these issues. So, in the spirit of increasing your chances of success and truly taking care of your customers, you need to focus on *both* solid engineering and professional design.

As a Business Leader, you choose whether to be intentional in using design to make your company more successful, or to let design self-regulate and cross your fingers that it doesn't do too much damage.

WHAT DESIGN IS AND ISN'T

Design is the intentional crafting of another person's experience. "Crafting," or exercising skill in making something, can be applied to everything from concepts as ethereal as "brand" to objects as tangible as signs. Crafting also applies to software products. When people think of software design, they often really mean "fonts and colors." But if you want to make an impact, you need to craft an entire *experience*. A Designer's job is to elicit intent from both businesses and users, and to craft the interactive and visual elements that will optimize the likelihood that people's experiences are as close to that intent as possible.

This book focuses on the software and product design of digital products. (Although they're related, advertising, marketing, and physical product design are outside its domain.) In 2000, Jesse-James Garrett introduced a fundamental model for digital product design in his book *The Elements of User Experience*. Every designer is familiar with this model. It differentiates between how things *look*, how they *act*, and *why* they exist in the first place.

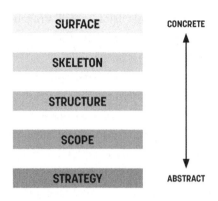

JESSE JAMES GARRETT'S MODEL OF THE ELEMENTS OF USER EXPERIENCE

According to Garrett's model, the design process works upwards from the bottom.

» **Strategy:** This is where it all begins—what is the opportunity and how might we take advantage of it? Strategy is sorted out under the leadership of Product Management, but it involves Design to help contribute, develop and test ideas.

» **Scope:** What must we address to have a product that's successful in the market? This is not about features, but rather what problems we must address for our customers.

» **Structure:** What are the necessary parts of the proposed solution, and how do they relate to one another? Getting this right is key to creating "intuitive" software whose value is self-evident.

» **Skeleton:** How is the solution instantiated in a navigation model, workflows and screens? Before getting into detail about the appearance of the product, this phase is for sorting out where and how information and functionality show up. Systems and patterns begin to be developed in this phase.

» **Surface:** Finally, how does the finished product look? More than just colors and fonts, this also addresses information hierarchy, clear calls to action, and detailed design systems.

Business Leaders who are unfamiliar with Design often only think about the top two layers of the model—how things *look*. They don't expect Designers to address how things *act. Why* comes up even less often: Who is this for? How and why will they use it? (Sometimes even Designers work too high up in the model, limiting and short-changing their potential contribution.) As a Business Leader, your greatest impact and value occur earlier in the design process, starting with expecting and encouraging Designers to work with you from the bottom up.

CHAPTER 1: HOW DESIGN ADDS VALUE TO YOUR BUSINESS

There is a LOT of available data demonstrating the value of design to businesses. Leah Buley, a former Forrester analyst and design strategist and practitioner, elegantly explains how design impacts business (parentheticals mine):

It makes employees more efficient and productive
(by helping to make decisions more quickly and with
better alignment, and freeing non-Designers from
design work),
which puts products in the market quicker (obviously)
that are more innovative (where design thinking
really shines)
and drives higher customer lifetime value (because
they better meet the needs of the market through
better understanding, better quality, and better testing
of ideas),
improving the company's market share and position and,
ultimately, leading to growth.

Several recent studies provide clear data supporting the
value of good design. McKinsey's 2018 "Business Value of Design"
report showed that companies with top-quartile McKinsey Design
Index Scores outperformed industry-benchmark growth by as
much as two to one across both total revenue and total returns to
shareholders. Forrester did an in-depth study of IBM's investment
in design and showed a 301% ROI over three years. A baseline
10% of projects either never reached the market or returned no
profit—that number was cut to 2% after IBM invested in design.
In other words, 8% of the projects that Product Managers and
Engineers lost sleep over could have been made successful or
pivoted (or tabled) sooner if design was part of the team.

Designers often don't learn about business, and aren't
expected to be conversant about business. **However, you can't
build a software company without design any more than you can
build one without code.** And if your Designers aren't speaking or
thinking business, it's hard to make them a meaningful part of
the team. They may be working towards fundamentally different

goals—and then you end up with arguments about Designers being "unrealistic perfectionists" who slow things down and get stuck on details. However, Designers are getting better at articulating the value of their work to the product and company. And as a Business Leader, it's your responsibility to build teams of design-valuing Product Managers, business-savvy Designers, and user-focused Engineers, all of whom understand their relationship to the health of the business.

A subpar user interface means you are squandering your Engineering resources. It doesn't matter how powerful your product is if its features are inaccessible because the user interface is awkward to use or impossible to understand. A company I worked with was paying for a product with the functionality they desperately needed, but its advanced features were too hard to figure out, so they only used the basic ones. Then, they switched to a competitor's product whose freemium model had better usability! Startups with great usability are eating the lunch of non-user-centric companies.

It's a waste of resources to pay Engineers and Product Managers to do design work. In engineering-dominated environments, you might hear, "There really isn't an interface." Translation: "The developers design the interface as they build." In other companies, Product Managers or Business Analysts might do design work. Why?

> » They don't know how to describe an impact, outcome, story, or feature without drawing it.
> » They don't know that design training and experience results in measurably better work.
> » They don't know that a designer should be (and is capable of) designing every little detail.
> » Over-the-counter prototyping tools make it too easy for them to approximate this work.

If your ratio of Designers to Engineers is very much lower than 1:8, you are almost certainly paying a non-Designer to do design work. *This is a complete waste of their time.* While some Engineers or PMs are skilled Designers, it is not likely they have the training or the perspective to step back from the code and look at their product as a typical user might.

As a rule, Engineers love computers; after all, they've chosen to spend their careers with them. This differentiates them from most people using their product. In his foundational book *The Inmates are Running the Asylum*, Alan Cooper jokingly classifies Engineers as *homo logicus*. Members of this species are different from *homo sapiens*; they're willing to trade simplicity for control, success for understanding, and what is probable for what is possible. And even if your product is *for* Engineers, your users aren't your developers. They don't know your product inside and out, they don't think about it constantly, and they don't care as much about it.

Product Managers shouldn't be doing design, either. They already have full-time jobs performing critical functions, which includes understanding and sizing the market, defining product opportunity and vision, and managing the business.

Resident experts produce better design work more efficiently. They also save your organization from the design-by-committee trap. I once listened in on a 37-minute conference call (no kidding; I timed it!) between five people trying to decide whether to use a pull-down list or radio buttons for a form on their interface. No one wants to be in—or pay for—these long, miserable, *expensive* meetings. Plus, the outcome is never optimal: after you release your subpar product, it will limp along or fail, and you'll have to rework it and start the cycle all over again.

THE DESIGN VALUE GAP

Two years ago, I ran a mini-workshop for 50 B2B CTOs and CIOs. I asked, "Who believes that design is critical to the success of their company? Show me 5 fingers if you feel it's true, 4 if it's mostly true, and so on." To my surprise, every single person held up 4 or 5 fingers (I expected at least one to argue that since their solution was built by Engineers for Engineers, they didn't need Designers). *Great,* I thought, *this will be a walk in the park.* Then, I shared the list of characteristics developed by the venture capital firm NEA in their *Future of Design in Startups Report* to define "design-centric" companies:

» Design integrated across multiple areas
» User-centricity
» Dedicated design team
» Designers as part of C-Level or Executive team
» A founder who is a designer
» Equal ratio of Designers to Engineers (!)

This list is EXTREMELY ambitious, and to be honest, I don't think an equal ratio of Designers to Engineers is even desirable— but I was stacking the deck. Next, I asked, "How many of you work for companies that have three of these characteristics?" All I got was one half-hearted wave. These organizations couldn't even say they were user-centric and that they had a dedicated design team! They all believed in the value of design, but they weren't putting any wood behind it. I'm afraid my astonishment offended some of them, but on reflection, it struck me that most companies wouldn't fare any better.

CHAPTER 2: BUILDING DESIGN CAPABILITIES

Now that we see some of the ways good design adds value to your organization, let's examine how to make your organization more capable of good design. This chapter will discuss hiring considerations to build internal design competency, as well as how and when to use external resources.

Design is under-represented in the tech space. To some degree, this is because software design as a discipline is late to the party. Engineering, quality assurance, and product management (or at least Business Leadership) all preceded design as formal roles on software product teams.

Design lags most significantly in the B2B space, which is still catching up to B2C's (business-to-consumer) adoption of design as a core competency. This gap exists because traditionally, the people who purchased B2B software weren't the people who used it. Companies selling software in the B2B world could be customer-centric without being user-centric. Additionally, when buyers closed the deal in the pre-SaaS (software-as-a-service) world, they were locked in, sometimes for years, regardless of subsequent complaints. People got used to using crappy software, and switching was costly. Today, most digital products and services are delivered "as a service." Business models have adapted; individual users can adopt B2B software, and then drive organizational adoption through a "grass roots" model.

At the same time, the design bar has been rising. B2C companies have to embrace design, because consumers can abandon their products if they aren't satisfied. Don't like Spotify? Switch to Pandora—it's one click away. And today, in what's being called the "consumerization of the enterprise," the same expectations for the quality of B2C user experience and design are being applied to B2B. In other words, B2B products are expected to have "consumer-grade" user experience design, because everyone who uses technology is accustomed to the experience quality of Apple and Google.

Hiring Designers isn't easy. Even junior Designers are in high demand. Consequently, lots of people ask whether to bring in an external design consultancy or hire and build an internal team.

The bottom line is that you should hire. Design is—and should be—a core competency. And in addition, you should consider external partnerships.

YES AND YES

Internal vs. external is not necessarily an either/or decision. Bring in a design partnership for the same reasons you'd bring in engineering help, a leadership coach, or a marketing consultant: to create a more effective team.

If you already have an internal design team, adding an external Partner (if managed well, and not in a frustrating or disenfranchising way) can work extremely well. You can use the Partner to:

» Support an initiative that's bigger than the standard workload, or fundamentally new.
» Introduce new skills or processes.
» Excite and engage the internal team.
» Amplify the design team's voice.

If you're trying to build a design team while meeting current design needs, bringing in a Partner while hiring in parallel has several additional advantages:

» You can move initiatives forward with strong design support and without waiting until a hire is complete and up to speed.
» An external Partner can introduce you to recruiters who "get it," review portfolios, help conduct interviews, and provide feedback.
» You demonstrate to potential hires that you care about design and are invested in it, literally.
» A well-respected external Partner, who can provide teaching and help, is a big draw for potential hires.

» When your internal designer(s) work with an
external Partner on a project, they'll understand
the background of each decision and will be able to
support and extend the design going forward. That
means you'll get more from the design work you
paid for.

CONSIDERATIONS WHEN MAKING INTERNAL HIRES

Look to your ratio of Engineers to Designers to understand the
gap between the investment and the opportunity represented
by bringing on design. Marty Cagan, a widely regarded thought
leader for technology product management, advocates a ratio of
1:8 Designers to Engineers. Depending on the complexity of the
product, the type of users, and the business, somewhere between
1:5 and 1:8 is probably an appropriate ratio. Expect salaries to
be roughly commensurate. And yet... the U.S. Bureau of Labor
Statistics reports that companies spend 30x more on engineering
than design.

You may need some experimentation to figure out the right
ratio, but here are some steps you can take:

1. Determine your current Designer-to-Engineer ratio.

2. Ask Designers, Product Management, and
   Engineering five questions:
   » What % of your time do you spend doing design
   work, aka making decisions about user experience?
   » How much of that time is spent alone vs. with
   people from the other two teams?
   » How much of that time is high-level vs. detailed?

» What do you think is our current Designer-to-Engineer ratio?

» What do you think is an appropriate ratio?

3. Assess what you learn, and adjust, using these rules of thumb:

» If Engineers and Product Managers spend more than 2% of their solo time doing high-level design work (the 2% accounts for research, thinking, and concepting), this is an obvious indicator that you need more Designers.

» Engineers and Product Managers should not regularly spend more than 5% of their solo time doing detailed design work.

» Engineers should spend at least 10% of their time in conversation with the Design team. If this is not happening, your Engineers or Designers may be too strapped for time or there may be a more complex partnership issue. If Product Managers spend less than 15% of their time collaborating with the Design team, you may have a similar problem as above.

» How does the current ratio compare to what employees think and want? A large misalignment is an indicator that things are way off.

4. Check in again after the changes have been in place for six months or so.

Knowing your ratio can be particularly helpful if you're also tracking other related things, like team satisfaction, NPS, or velocity, so that you can start to understand any correlation. It also suggests a budget source if you're having trouble funding Designers. If hiring six Engineers will throw off your ratio, perhaps hire five, and use that sixth headcount for a Designer.

Don't try to find a unicorn, someone who can write front-end code *and* do visual design for your website *and* do all the product interaction design. You're rarely hiring both a Front-End Developer and a Designer in one person. Moreover, a Designer will have expertise in Advertising and Marketing or Product, but usually not both. And finally, a Product Designer will be better at either Interaction Design or Visual Design. A job description requesting one person to fill all these positions will make you look like a novice. List and prioritize the work you need help with. Then see how it fits within the job titles described below.

Job titles in software design have been a mess. Happily, the trend seems to be settling into the following few areas:

Design Manager: Design Managers also may be called Art Directors, Creative Directors, Design Leads, and/or Design Directors. Art Directors and Creative Directors are more common in advertising or marketing. Design Leads usually are senior Designers responsible for day-to-day work on a project, with one or more other Designers assigned. Within a leadership team, you may also find a Director or VP of Design or Customer Experience, or, less often, a Chief Design Officer. Obviously, the higher up Design is in your organization, the bigger strategic impact they can have. Tactically, you will need a manager once you get to a 4– or 5–person design team.

Visual Designer (VisD): Also called Interface Design, User Interface Design (how the thing looks, as opposed to how it acts in Interaction Design), or UI Design, this role owns the top layer of JJG's model (Surface), and collaborates with Interaction Design on the second layer (Skeleton). They are responsible for the visual language of the product, including hierarchy of information and clarity of available actions. A senior Visual Designer comes up with ideas about visual design direction, nails down the final visual system, and applies it to key screens. Junior Visual Designers apply and extend the system to other pages and elements.

Interaction Designer (IxD): Interaction Designers map to the bottom four layers of JJG's model, working closely with Product Management, Engineering, Visual Design, and Research. They are responsible for understanding what users are trying to accomplish, what's technically feasible, and how that might fit in with the business. Then, they create workflows and basic screens (wireframes) that describe how the software will work. Senior IxDs come up with big ideas, organizing concepts, and key workflows and screens. Junior IxDs extend the concepts and patterns to new workflows.

A "Product Designer" is an Interaction Designer at heart (they can do all the interaction design necessary to describe a digital product), and is reasonably competent at visual design.

Most of the time, depending on the product differentiators, users, and value proposition, I recommend prioritizing Interaction Design over Visual Design. It has a bigger impact in terms of product usability, it often varies widely screen to screen, and, given the visual design libraries available today, it's harder to fake.

User Experience Designer (UXD): UXD is the umbrella term for the entire discipline. It's often used interchangeably with Interaction Designer, especially juxtaposed with UI, as in, "We have three UX Designers and one UI designer." Since many people use UX in their title, measure their ability by their years of relevant experience. Adjacent titles that *sound* like UXD are commonly used in digital marketing/advertising design, such as Digital/Interactive Art Director, Creative Director, and Interactive Designer; these are not equivalent.

Researcher: Although you probably won't need this role right away, it's great to have a Researcher (also known as a Usability or User Researcher) in-house. Relying on external Research partners makes it tempting to run fewer, bigger studies; this is the opposite of how you want to learn. Researchers should contribute at every layer of JJG's model. They provide generative ("feed-forward") research in advance of making any artifacts, and feedback after the fact. If you have three or four Designers on staff, you probably have enough work for a Researcher. They will help generate new ideas, test ideas early and often (before you spend money on development), and compare what actually gets built with your competitors' products. Even a single staff Designer should be spending part of their time doing research alongside your Product Manager.

Many Designers are skilled Moderators, meaning they're trained in and experienced at talking to users. Moderation is part of the research process, but designing, synthesizing, organizing, and making research available to others is necessary, too. A Lead Researcher can lean on Designers to do moderation, thus extending your research capabilities. However, someone skilled at moderation may not have the skills or bandwidth to lead research. Talk with your Designers and Researchers to identify your staff's skills and where the team is lacking.

UX Writer: A relatively recent title, the UX writer creates the copy and "microcopy" within your product. That includes instructions, help text, field names, error messages, button names, and any other words that a user might see. As most teams aren't large enough to warrant a full-time UX writer, this job most commonly falls to Designers, often with feedback from research and QA, and with varying degrees of success.

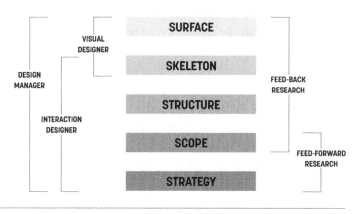

DESIGN ROLES AND TYPES OF RESEARCH APPLIED TO THE "ELEMENTS" MODEL

The Designer-to-Engineer ratio I discussed earlier is a blunt-force tool. It's also important to evaluate how many of each type of design resource you need. Very complex tools and workflows require more Interaction Designers and Researchers. If you run a large eCommerce site, you might invest in more Research and Visual Design. A simple workflow or a startup B2C focused on younger users requires higher initial investment in Visual Design. There are some rules of thumbs for ratios within a design organization:

> » Unless you're a tiny company, your team should have at least 1 Interaction Designer per Visual Designer, one (or both) of whom has research training and experience.

> » A complex product (nearly all B2B products, and B2C products in spaces like healthcare or finance) requires a ratio that's closer to 3–4 Interaction Designers: 1 Visual Designer: 1 Researcher.

INTERVIEWING

You can rely heavily on a Design Partner (or an Advisor) to help in the hiring process. If you don't have a Design Partner, or if your organization is small, you'll want to participate in interviews, as well. Much of what you already know about hiring holds for Designers, but there are a few additional things to look for:

> » Does their actual resume look great? Is it easy to read? If section divisions are unclear, if the font size is odd or the lines are smashed together, if there are sloppy errors—don't interview them. Their first design assignment was to make a resume that their target audience (you) understands and appreciates. It is entirely appropriate to use your personal judgement here.

» Are they interested in other aspects of your company? Asking about your technology stack, your go-to-market strategy, or your business model shows a well-rounded individual. Look for someone who understands they're using their design skillset to solve business problems.

» Consider the aesthetics of their portfolio. Don't worry too much about being subjective—your subjective opinion matters!

- *Is it current?* For example, are there shadows and gradients where most things you see today are flat, corners where you mostly see curves, bold colors where most palettes are muted?

- *Is it consistent?* For example, does the shade of blue change from one screen to another? Do the page titles change size?

- *Is it neat?* For example, do things line up with each other? Can you understand what's happening on a screen?

- *Is it attractive?* This one is simple: do you like how it looks?

  If the answer to any of these questions is "no," ask about what you're seeing. They should be able to have an open, non-defensive conversation, and you should take the chance to learn the rationales behind their choices. After all, who knows? Maybe research on 17-year-olds revealed that that particular shade of hot pink is irresistible. And once you have other Designers on staff, they can help assess portfolios.

» How do they take criticism? Ask about something in their portfolio. It doesn't really matter what—ask why the background isn't yellow, or why the button is on the top instead of the bottom. A defensive or deflective reaction is cause for concern. ("My CEO insisted." "That would never work." "Huh. Maybe.") Responding with a question gets an A+. ("Interesting. Why would you make it yellow?") Look for openness to discussion. How Designers listen to and incorporate other people's ideas is critical for your organization. I ignored this rule one time. The Designer I hired was even more defensive and resistant once she was on the job; our subsequent painful conversations and eventual parting of ways burned this lesson into my skull. Never, ever hire someone who doesn't take criticism well in the interview.

» When sharing their portfolio, are they clear and specific about what they did versus what someone else on their team did? Collaboration is common; it's likely that other people contributed to the work. You want someone who embraces collaborators, or at least doesn't hog all the credit! You also want to be clear on what the Designer contributed and what someone else did.

» Can they talk clearly about the process of developing their pieces? Their process—how they think and approach problem-solving—actually is more important than their result, which for example, could mostly be the product of the CEO's input.

» Does their academic degree suggest someone who can be a creative systems thinker who can work within constraints? I've had great luck hiring people whose formal education was in Architecture,

Industrial Design, or Engineering, followed by additional training in Interaction or Visual Design.

» Finally, how do they think? I like to talk Designers through a small, real challenge we're currently facing to see how they react and what their thought process is. Hopefully, they jump up to the whiteboard and start drawing and asking questions. And again, the final output isn't really what matters; rather, assess how they think and how they work.

PUTTING YOUR BEST FOOT FORWARD

In addition to standard considerations, you should be aware of some things that Designers look for in a prospective employer:

» **Design advocacy and investment.** Senior Executives at the company who believe in what design can do for their success, have a vision for how that will happen, and advocate for investing in design.

» **Other Designers.** Developers stuck trying to fix a bug often turn to online communities for help. These communities also exist for Designers, but nothing compares with being able to turn and chat with your neighbor. 25% of our Designers joined our studio because they were tired of being singletons in their organizations; they wanted to collaborate with and learn from other Designers.

» **Pleasant physical space.** Design centers and consultancies alike invest in polished concrete floors, natural light, and Eames chairs on the reasonable premise that Designers appreciate good design. You're competing with companies providing these kinds of spaces. And since your Designers should not be physically separated from their product teams, Engineers, or Product Managers, this investment will improve the space for everyone!

» **Specialized hardware and software.** Bigger monitors, up-to-date drawing tools like interactive pen displays or pen tablets, and top-of-the-line hardware and software products.

SALARIES

The ROI of hiring a Designer should be clear and easy to support if you understand how they'll contribute to your company's success. A skilled Interaction Designer is roughly equivalent to the cost of an Engineer, and the same salary variations apply based on geography, trendy titles, and new degrees. The Creative Group / Robert Half Technologies, O'Reilly's Design Salaries Survey, and Glassdoor publish good salary surveys.

ONBOARDING

Hiring one (or a few) Designers doesn't mean your job is done. They need to be working closely with Product Management and Engineering. Unfortunately, I see too many companies where execs heard that design could make their business more successful (yay!), hired a Designer or two (yay!), and then disengaged (boo!).

My company holds "office hours" for the portfolio companies of venture capital firms, where we discuss some design problem they're having. This can cover everything from how to hire designers to improving conversion on checkout to reviewing an entire product and providing overall feedback. Normally, companies send their CXO or a VP, along with the appropriate staff. But in one particularly poignant session, the lone Designer of a 300-person company was the only one who came to the meeting. This was the first warning sign that the CEO (who'd been personally invited by their VC) didn't consider design to be important. In fact, users were having significant difficulties with their complex B2B product; clearly, design *was* important but not prioritized by the organization.

The Designer told us he'd dropped into a meeting between QA and Engineering where they were arguing about the best way to show a specific feature. After listening carefully, he asked, "Was there something about my design that didn't work?' "What??" asked the Engineer, shocked. "I had no idea you'd already designed this! Where is it?"

Someone in this organization had gotten approval for a single Designer. However, since the Designer-to-Engineer ratio hovered around 1:100, his contribution was so anomalous and scattershot that it usually was missed altogether. The Engineers were used to doing the design work themselves! Without executive support, this Designer was doomed. I recommended he find a new gig.

CONSIDERATIONS WHEN SELECTING DESIGN PARTNERS / VENDORS

A Design Partner can have a massive, fast, positive impact for their clients and their clients' customers. Vendors specialize in a variety of sizes and engagement styles, so it's critical to hire the right kind of Design Partner.

Types of Design Partners

Freelancer (a single person): Hiring an individual freelancer is a great way to start. Request that they work on-site with your team, and ask for references to other freelancers with skills that complement theirs when needed.

Boutique (a handful of staff): A small group of design practitioners who generally have a narrow focus like health care, non-profits, or cloud storage.

Design Studio (20+ staff): A design-centered company with specialized roles like research, interaction, visual UI, and prototyping. They should have deep experience in some specific verticals; they should have a collaborative and iterative design process and focus on outcomes (not deliverables); and they should have some ability to train and level up your team.

Digital Agency (100+ staff): These agencies are "full service"; their large programs encompass business, design, and technology. They often focus on traditional industries like entertainment, finance, or consumer goods, and have added digital as a new channel for their existing products and services.

Consultancy (Hundreds of staff): Many consultancies are adding digital design capabilities, often through acquisition: Accenture acquired Fjord, McKinsey acquired Veryday, and Capgemini acquired Idean.

Be creative in considering how your Partner might help you. They may integrate and level-up a design resource you currently have, help the whole organization with process best practices, or help establish a vision.

Engagement Styles

There are many options for engaging with vendors. Find the style that maps to your specific project needs, not the style that maps best to the consultancy's business model.

Staff augmentation provides temporary dedicated resources who work onsite like full-time employees.

Project-based work includes an upfront definition of schedule, milestones, phase types, and activities/deliverables. A "fixed fee" for services, along with additional fees and overages, are accounted for in a detailed Statement of Work (SOW).

Agile engagements or retainers eschew milestones and deliverables, relying on a sprint schedule for scope. Cost is calculated by determining resources and the potential number of sprints multiplied by a rate card. This type of engagement lowers the upfront detail in the SOW, using an agile process like "scrum" to plan.

Outcome-based design focuses on a desired outcome and the value of the opportunity the work represents. This is not a very common engagement type, but I hope it will continue to grow, as it forces the Design Partner's goals into alignment with yours.

I recommend starting with a project-based engagement with a fixed fee and deliverables that would be useful to you even if the engagement ends. This gives everyone a chance to get to know one another and understand scope and expectations. Then, move to a sprint- and outcome-based retainer if your organization is at all agile.

QUESTIONS TO ASK CONSULTANCIES

Before you agree to a project, ask these questions of a prospective agency:

» *Given our deadline and our own internal processes, how would you implement continuous iteration and testing out concepts and designs with users?*
The best design isn't a single event; it's an ongoing process of incremental steps. How does the agency include iteration and testing within their process, and how will they adjust to fit with yours? Wrong answers include: "Just follow our process, that's what you're hiring us for," and "It's impossible to test in this timeframe."

» *How and when do you incorporate research?*
Good Designers are excited about the opportunity to learn from others, including not just users but also subject matter experts (SMEs) and stakeholders. Look for interesting ideas about who to talk to (not just the usual suspects), a desire to learn from you and your colleagues, and a plan for sharing what they learn inclusively and engagingly.

» *Do your consultants have experience working on internal design teams?*
It's easier to work with a designer who has experienced different processes and can adapt to yours. Look for consultancies where a good portion of the staff (and the team you'll be working with) have spent much of their career internally.

» *Who will I be working with?*
Unfortunately, it's very common to not work with the person you first meet. But even if you don't have a firm start date, ask for who your team might be, and then confirm who they actually are once the start date is nailed down.

» *How will we work together?*
How will we manage meetings, documents, and communications? How often will we meet in person? There is no one "right" answer, but you need to feel comfortable with whatever is discussed.

» *Can you show me Key Performance Indicators from other successful projects? How does your work impact your clients' businesses? How would we establish our success metrics for this project?*
You'll glean from their answers whether they understand or care about this. Interestingly, our clients often don't want to put success metrics and baselines in place because the work we do with them is so complex and has so many dependencies, but ideally, you should be prepared to help the consultancy measure your shared success.

» *Can you show me examples of work in progress?*
Ask to see more than just the end deliverables. Examine case studies or work samples from three projects that align with your own. Look for intersections in client size, target market, project goal, domain, or complexity.

» *Where will you end the process?*
You're looking for people who will stick with you through launch, not just through some limited set of

deliverables that they'll get paid for. Their stopping-point should be based on your needs, process, and success, in consultation with your engineering team. If you are agile, they should support your sprints through release. Ideally, the vendor builds some flexibility into their SOW so that a prototype handoff can be scheduled later in the process.

» *How will knowledge transfer work when you're done?* In addition to the final deliverables, how can your company learn, adopt best practices, and extend the design? What collaboration, training, or documentation will take place? You both are working to create value beyond this single product design, so you don't lose design expertise when the external team leaves.

» *How much of what you design actually gets released*? Very few vendors will be able to answer this question, but they may be able to ball-park it. Much of the actual release is usually out of their control—but not all of it. Hire someone who cares and talks about how they ensure their work contributes to their clients' success.

» *What don't you do?* Even if they do it all, they're probably still better at one thing than another. Investigate their history and make sure they are true digital product Designers.

» *What will you need from us?* Savvy clients ensure that they understand what will be expected of them beyond the money—time, energy, political support, and introductions are all common, but by no means an exhaustive list.

SPEC WORK

Many companies, whether hiring individuals or consultancies, ask for spec work during the interview or sales process. Spec work is when you send candidates or vendors away with assignments to complete as part of the assessment process. Doing work "on spec" (on speculation of being hired) is a hot topic in the design world. One quick Google search returns hundreds of hits—ranging from anti-spec statements by professional organizations to on-point, angry, and hilarious blog posts slamming prospective employers who want it. This is what Designers may think of when you ask them to do spec work, so unless you're the gorilla of your domain, I advise against it. The process designers use for spec work rarely resembles the work you will pay them to do later. It's a false task that will get you false results.

COMMON PUSHBACKS

Congratulations! You've made it. You understand and can explain the value of design and how you expect it to impact your company. You know what kind of design work you need to accomplish your goals, and what kind of Designers you want to hire. So far, so good. But you still need to convince your bosses or colleagues, who may have these common misconceptions:

We don't have anything to design.

Your counter: If a user interacts with anything digital, then *someone* is designing that experience (interaction design) and how it looks (user interface). And that someone is not a designer.

For example, tools built for Engineers often have a black-background text-only "command-line interface" (CLI). I nearly always hear companies say, "That's just a CLI; we don't need a design for that." However, it's precisely when there's nothing but a limited toolkit for design options that a trained Designer may be the MOST needed!

I recently conducted usability research on an extremely popular developer tool. We were testing to see if engineers understood whether a file they were retrieving would meet their needs. Considerations included telling them the size of the file, whether it was official or certified for various uses, and when it was best to give them that information to ensure they didn't waste time with files that wouldn't work for them. After we redesigned it, changing just a few colors, letter case, and information location, mistaken downloads were significantly reduced and user happiness was significantly increased.

The counter to this "we don't have design" argument simple. Pull up whatever your buyers or customers interact with, whether it's an ATM kiosk, a command-line interface, or the "GUI," and point out that someone decided how it would look and act. That is design.

We don't need Designers because we I know what our users want.

Welcome to the "Steve Jobs Theory of Design." Your counter: Jobs *did* say, "It's really hard to design products by focus groups. A lot of times, people don't know what they want until you show it to them." However, it's a misinterpretation to suggest that he had disdain for anything but his own opinion. In fact, he was referring specifically to marketing (truly, watch the video).

Steve Jobs did not do solo genius design. If he thought he could, he wouldn't have assembled the best design team in the industry.

We don't need Designers because our users are just like us.

Your counter: Unless all of your users work at your company, and even if your users are Engineers, they're not just like you. They don't live and breathe your product; they're less invested than you are. Moreover, understanding your users' goals and tasks doesn't mean that you are adept at designing to support them. Besides, look at GitHub. As of the date of publication, they had 20+ Designers on staff—and if there ever was an argument for "our users are just like us," GitHub would be it.

We don't need Designers because our Product Managers do the design.

"The product or domain is too complicated"; "Product Managers are responsible for the P&L so they should be responsible for the design"; "This saves us money."
Your counter: Assigning Design to your Product Managers is a waste of money. The time they spend struggling to design a product could be better spent talking to users, assessing competitors, understanding legal and regulatory issues, and doing the other things that they are experts at (and responsible for).

Designers won't understand this product; it's too complicated.

The underlying assumption here is that Designers are not as technically-minded as anyone else in the organization. Your counter: This just isn't the case. Design Consultancies are experts at getting up to speed quickly on new products, technologies, and domains. Internal hires should demonstrate the same level of intelligence that you expect from Sales, Support, Engineering, or any other employee who needs to understand your product.

Design will slow us down.

Your counter: Design actually should *increase* your trajectory, by freeing Product Management and Engineering from time-consuming tasks they're not well-suited for. Design dramatically reduces waste by speeding decision-making, improving your organizations' ability to learn from users, and creating more usable products. A New Enterprise Associates study found that 75% of the most deeply-design-committed companies described *faster* product cycles as a result of their skilled design teams. More importantly, using Design effectively reduces risk and increases the speed at which you find solutions that resonate with users and the larger market. Marty Cagan calls this phenomenon "time to money," as opposed to "time to market."

Design is too expensive.

Your counter: Design should pay for itself, and easily. If Designers are doing their work, then everyone else is doing theirs. We can focus on the best possible options for our users so that we're more profitable, more quickly, and at lower cost.

It's too early for us to need design.

Your counter: If you are discussing who your users are, what their goals are, and how you might help them accomplish your goals, then it's not too early. Designers can talk to users, synthesize and illustrate consensus, and, most importantly, design prototypes to describe and test ideas. Since they'll be designing from the beginning and developing and discarding ideas with the rest of the team, ramp-up time will not be a factor; you won't find yourself waiting mid-stream to get somebody on board. In short, bringing design in earlier will get you to money faster.

CHAPTER 3: THE DESIGN PROCESS AND GIVING INPUT

When I give Business Leaders a list of our training topics, they're almost always interested in learning how to give useful feedback. It turns out that no one ever showed them how to do it well. Giving design feedback is scary because it calls for design knowledge (similarly, most would be anxious to give feedback on a Developer's code) and it's usually done in a group setting.

However, Business Leaders must provide initial direction (Hugh Dubberly calls this feed-*forward*, direction coming before anything is designed), as opposed to feed-*back*, which happens after something is designed. This chapter describes how to provide input at each step of the design process:

1. Feed-forward (providing initial direction)

2. Process and Deliverables (doing the design)

3. Feed-back (assessing and responding to the design)

FEED-FORWARD   FEED-BACKWARD
(INTERVIEW-BASED)   (TEXT-BASED)

In this type of research you'll   Here you will have more
have more Open-Ended   task-based questions and
Questions, informing your   activities, informing your
future product ideas   existing product ideas

YOUR PRODUCT IDEA

FEED-FORWARD: VISION AND SCOPE

The most crucial thing a Business Leader can provide a Designer (and, indeed, a team) is **vision**. The vision describes the opportunity, the constraints that a solution must take into account, and the desired outcome. Your team depends on you to understand the market, competitors, constraints, and business opportunity. When you clearly and enthusiastically communicate your vision of how we might address and take advantage of all those things, then your team can bring their imagination, skills, energy, and experience to bear.

What Not to Do: The Theory of Napkins

As a Business Leader, you pose the question, "How might we take advantage of this opportunity?" Leverage and collaborate with your design team on the details of how to address your vision. Don't *dictate* to them. If you already have the whole solution in your head in the guise of "requirements," and you believe your design team is just there to make it look pretty, you risk going too far into defining the product. This causes three big problems:

1. You are working outside your area of expertise

2. You are not leveraging your Designers' expertise

3. You discourage your staff

To illustrate: In a scene in the (alas, canceled) television show *Smash,* an inexperienced Director tells the leading lady how to say her line. Theater is an old profession with a well-established etiquette, and being given a "line reading" is considered demeaning. The underlying message is: "Your value is in your ability to mimic me."

Most Designers know this feeling. A colleague, boss, or client drops by with something they've scribbled on a napkin and asks, "Can you just take this concept and make it pretty?" This is the equivalent of a line reading. It's what I call "giving a napkin"— the outline of a solution that kills your team's ability to make a meaningful contribution. To be clear: *drawing a sketch is great if it's the beginning of a conversation. If it's the end, then you've delivered a napkin. In that case, you're only getting 10% of the value of your Designers.* This is true whether it's a napkin, a whiteboard sketch, a wireframe, or finished code with a "roughed out" interface.

Everyone in the world has received a "napkin." It could be a broad hint about what to get for an anniversary, a vision that came to the CEO in the shower that now you as Product Manager are stuck implementing, or your kid's letter to Santa. My hairstylist friend has clients who demand a specific cut, even after he tells them it'll be impossible with their hair—disregarding his experience and training. He wonders if they need so little guidance from him, why don't they go somewhere less expensive? He's getting a napkin. I've met Designers who have quit their jobs because they got nothing but napkins.

If you think you give napkins, there is an easy fix. Go ahead and sketch up your idea. Then, sit with the Designer and discuss it! Explain your choices—"I added this big photo of a car because I think our competitor's site really appeals to auto enthusiasts." This does two things. It shows that you're not intending for them to just prettify your idea. And it opens up a conversation so your Designer can explore your goals and work with you on more (and better!) ideas for solutions.

What Also Not to Do: The Anti-Napkin

In my conversations with Designers, another pattern has emerged: the anti-napkin. In these scenarios, the concept is overly-broad, and the strategy is weak, unknown, or absent. A friend of mine recently got an anti-napkin assignment: "Design a social networking application for our grad students. We need it to be sticky... lots of traffic and engagement. Can't wait to see what you come up with!" My friend received little information about the goals or technical constraints of the application, just that a competitor was doing something similar and the university didn't want to be left behind.

This kind of request can be born out of a questionable business case—there are no constraints, and no real opportunities for success, because there are unclear or specious goals. It also can come from a desire to be generous with "fun" assignments and give the Designer "freedom." However, Designers are bounded problem-solvers. Constraints generally inspire creativity.

In fact, this is true for everyone. According to several studies, working with a scarcity of resources, or even *thinking* about scarcity, causes people to be more creative. Don't anti-napkin your design team. Provide them with a vision that describes your goals, the opportunity, the risks that worry you, the legal, regulatory, budget, and brand constraints, and any concerns you have. They should be able to work with you and ask questions to help you all better understand the boundaries to the problem (certainly there are some, unless you're offering $1000 to everyone who visits your site—that would make it sticky!).

I realize that I've said, "Don't give too much detail. Also, don't give too little." So where's the sweet spot? What makes teams feel excited, invested in, valued, creative? I asked 30 Designers, "What's the best product description you've ever received from a Business Leader?" I searched for some pattern in the resulting collection of spreadsheets, one-pagers, business model canvases, and story-maps. Unfortunately, the only theme that emerged was: "It depends." It depends on the Business Leader, the Designer, their experience working together, their experience in the domain, and many more factors. However, it's a good start to realize that providing too much or too little detail to your Design team can seriously limit the value of their contribution. Ask for their input. I've seen teams improve collaboration and significantly reduce frustration through conscious conversation.

Design to Support Your Vision

As a Leader, you feed-forward, providing initial vision and direction. A design team will often do early thought work as well, and create documents that confirm alignment with, provide perspective on, or add detail to their understanding of your vision. Design teams drive the creation of these documents, but it's critical that you help shape them. This section captures a list of common examples, but your team may create different things. (You can also ask them about creating one or two of these.)

Manifestos or Design Principles

In 1998, the original TiVo design team famously wrote a manifesto that began with: "It's entertainment, stupid." It went on:

» It's TV, stupid
» It's video, damnit
» Everything is smooth and gentle
» No modality or deep hierarchy
» Respect the viewer's privacy
» It's a robust appliance, like a TV

Its manifesto led TiVo to ditch old-school remotes, hunt-and-peck technology, and a utilitarian approach to tasks. Based on customer feedback, TiVo later revised its manifesto to remove all the "stupids" and update the focus—highlighting reliability, for example—but kept the point about entertainment. Manifestos with cross-feature and cross-product values help create a cohesive product and ease decision-making.

Personas

Personas are archetypal users generated after observing real-world patterns of goals and behaviors. Designers have employed user personas , which focus on the use of the product, as a best practice since at least 1998 (as opposed to marketing personas, which focus mainly on the selection and purchase of the product). Design and Research teams lead the creation of personas, but as a best practice, they bring along the larger team key points in the process and for research sessions. It is the Product Manager or Business Leader who selects a Primary and Secondary Persona, and explains the rationale for doing so, setting a clear north star for the team. They are saying, "This is who we're working for and what they need."

Storyboards

Storyboards are a wonderful opportunity for Business Leaders, Engineers, and Designers to collaborate. You spend time together discussing the world as it is today, how people experience it, and then the world of the future. The design team helps you think through and represent your story in pictures; they capture attention and specify the goal of your vision, without getting mired in the details. Include Engineers; they'll leverage their technical expertise and come up with new ideas that no one else knows are possible, and they'll provide early feasibility checks.

Visual Design Direction

Before starting visual design, you should be able to give some initial direction in a variety of areas:

> *The relationship between product design and your company's marketing guidelines or brand standards.* Generally Marketing will provide a logo and brand guidelines, but what freedom does the Product Design team have beyond that? Is the Marketing team flexible about extending the colors or using a more device-friendly font? Support your product design team in their conversations with Marketing.

The feeling you want users to have.
For example, "I can trust this product; it's solid, like a
bank." Or, "This is exciting technology, really cutting
edge."

The adjectives describing the product.
Avoid adjectives whose opposites are nonsensical.
For example, it might be nice to have a "clean" and
"modern" product, but nobody is asking for something
that's "dirty" or "old-school." Use more helpful
adjectives: feature-rich (vs. simple), luxury (vs. value-
focused), or information-rich (vs. does the heavy lifting
for you).

Other products, websites, packaging, or anything else
that you like, and why.
Curating a collection of these will help you see patterns
and assess things more critically.

Early Prototypes

Early prototypes can be created entirely by the Designers. Their
ability to do this quickly so that the team can all see, share, and
revise ideas is an important means of managing risk.

Early prototypes rarely have any real data; they look
polished enough to get the idea across, and only represent a few
workflows. However, because they look and to some degree even
act like real software, they are an integral part of Product Discovery.
They are rapid representations of how a concept or strategy *might*
be instantiated in a software product. Quick prototypes give the
team a chance to show executives, buyers, and users a reasonable
facsimile of the product idea with minimal investment. In this way,
you can learn a lot about how much users will value the proposed

product and whether they can use it with minimal cost. Designer-generated prototypes also reduce the risk that a proposed product will not be technically feasible, because Engineering has a very clear understanding of the idea. Early prototypes illuminate the power and the limitations of your ideas, often giving rise to new and better ones.

PROCESS AND DELIVERABLES: DOING DESIGN

At its most basic, design is a process of going wide and then narrowing, often more than once, to reach an optimal solution. Coming up with multiple solutions, weighing their merits, and then iterating the one you select are the hallmarks of "Design Thinking."

Briefly, Designers will go through these steps:

Learning > Ideating > Refining > Delivering

The length, order, and interaction between these steps varies widely from organization to organization. Your design team will adjust their methods and tools depending on the type of issue, risk, customer, and problem they're working with, but this broad framework is a good starting point.

Learning

Learning must take place throughout the design process. But there is usually some up-front contextual learning that needs to happen when designing a new significant feature or product. Learning *activities* can include talking to users and potential users (generative/feed-forward research), collecting available usage and support data, talking with the Product Manager and Engineering, and looking at competitors and adjacent or orthogonal products.

The *timeframe* for learning can be anywhere from a few days to several weeks or even months. Talking to users should never stop, but a big up-front research project can slow things down. Most of the time, it's more appropriate to encourage your design team to take a bit of time up- front (a few weeks max), and commit to allowing time for more learning throughout.

It's important to include Product Management and Engineering leadership in this phase so that everyone gains understanding of the users and the opportunity space.

Deliverables you might see during the learning phase include:

> » **Models:** Diagrams of the parts of a system or even an entire domain of knowledge and their relationships. These allow the team to understand, reflect, and collaborate on the product, system or topic being modeled.
> » **Protocols:** Loose scripts to guide discussions between Designers, product managers, or researchers, and users. (At this point, conversations should be pretty general. Later in the process, protocols will become lengthier and more prescriptive.)
> » **Research findings:** These may take the form of videos, personas, diagrams, notes, or reports. They synthesize what your researchers learned from users, subject matter experts, or internal teams like support, IT, or sales. All research conversations should be recorded and attended by one or two other folks.

Ideating

Ideating should be integrated with learning, and I'll get some raised eyebrows within the design community for separating them, but I'm doing so for simplicity. At some point, people on the team (not just Designers) will begin to have ideas for addressing business and user needs. Although ideating should be integrated with learning, there are some specific *ideating activities* (running workshops, for example) to conceive and refine ideas together with Engineering and Product Management. Do not let the design team disappear, devise grand schemes on their own, and hide their work until they've revised and polished it—their artifacts should be developed in concert with the larger team. My best products have emerged from close collaboration between Designers, Engineers, and Business Leaders. This is where the truly valuable, capital-D Design happens.

The *timeframe* for ideating can be anywhere from a few hours to days or weeks. Designers usually want more time for ideation (one reason people complain about design slowing things down). Encourage your team to involve others in their ideation, and to think of it as a lean process. As explained by Eric Ries, a core principle of the lean process is to accelerate the build-measure-learn feedback loop. The team should constantly be asking, "What's the least work we can do to learn what we need to know?" When the rest of the team sees rapid and valuable learning occurring, and compelling ideas being generated, it won't feel like a waste of time

Loosely, learning + ideation = "discovery." At times, these up-front steps can feel overly lengthy, giving some people the impression that design itself takes too long. But like learning, ideation should happen throughout the process—provided you make the bigger strategic and directional decisions first. Discovery actually *can* happen incredibly quickly, even several rounds in a single day, if you are focused on what you're trying to learn and the most efficient way to learn it.

The *artifacts* generated during Discovery are similar to the artifacts from other phases, but they are quick (inexpensive) renderings, fewer in number, less detailed, and unrefined.

» Literal sketches, on whiteboards or paper, are important tools in this phase. Sketches can describe concepts, screens, or workflows. If there are no sketches at all, the team may not be generating enough ideas; or they may be spending too much time rendering (i.e. investing in) unviable concepts.

» Wireframes are simple screen mockups, showing important information and functionality, and a suggested hierarchy. They're usually black and white, although sometimes a few colors indicate key elements. Wireframes are becoming less common as new tools make it easy to go straight to mockups. But quick digital sketches still can be useful for exploring and communicating ideas.

» Scenarios, Storyboards, or Workflows may be written, sketched storyboards (like a movie storyboard), or minimally labeled boxes connected by arrows, representing screens.

» Mockups, also called comps, are color pictures of screens; they look more realistic than wireframes. Mockups shouldn't be perfectly ideated, but they appear real enough to make it easy for people to imagine using the product.

» Prototype development obviously continues in the Discovery phase for the same reason they were developed in early phases: to manage risk. They can be as simple as mockups stitched together to make it appear like you can click from one screen to another. Some prototypes may be quite low-tech; others may be well-validated enough to benefit from having real data behind them. Today's tools make prototyping easy. Making the right prototype is a question of figuring out what you need to learn, and what is the least amount of work necessary to learn it. Use your Designers' prototypes to manage risk—to share information with stakeholders, get user feedback, and, later in the process, communicate to Engineering teams about the product and workflow.

Refining

There is no clear line between ideating and refining. But at some point, you'll hit on an idea that you want to move beyond sketches and prototypes—and this idea needs to be refined. During the refining phase, Designers improve on ideas based on feedback from potential users, partners, and stakeholders; post-ideation fine-tuning; and technical feasibility. They also add details, like screens and workflows outside the "big idea" developed in ideation. If this phase sounds troublingly vague to you, you're right. The time set aside for refining is like the suitcase you pack for vacation: you'll always fill up any extra space. Keep this phase productive by:

> **Talking to users.** Don't let something that tests well early in ideation lose its appeal somewhere along the refinement process. I saw this happen to a team that had a great core idea for a complex product. As they added the detailed controls necessary to actually use the product, the core interaction popular in ideation gradually got watered down. Luckily, the team caught the issue in time, and moved most of the controls to a "detail" screen. This let their big idea continue to shine.

> **Protecting refinement time.** When I ask Business Leaders what concerns them most about Designers, most say, "perfectionism"—and they're usually thinking of the refinement phase. However, it's very common for

Designers to hear that some issue with the UX or UI will be addressed in v2, only to find themselves reassigned and v2 time never materializing. If they see refinement time being aggressively shortened or removed, you can expect Designers to hoard time during Ideation. Remember: Designers see and improve things that you may not notice. This work is valuable. Polish creates an overall sense of professionalism.

Being prepared to make bold calls. The team is counting on you for this. Whether it's small revisions, massive pivots, or even scrapping ideas, your willingness to learn and make these decisions is crucial for product success.

Delivering

Collaboration between design teams and Engineers is key to delivering your product.

If you were able to involve a Lead Engineer in the first phases of the project, so they could help develop ideas based on their knowledge of what's possible, and so that they already have a good idea about what's coming, things will go much more smoothly during delivery. (The only exception to this rule is if you don't have an Engineer who thinks broadly and with enthusiasm about new ideas. If they focus on edge-cases and perceive their value as identifying risk rather than innovating, they probably will be counter-productive.) But in this phase, of course, the larger engineering team will be involved.

It's critical for Engineers and Designers to have a respectful, positive, even friendly relationship. They should sit close together if possible; they should have opportunities to socialize at work.

It doesn't matter how good the design is if it doesn't get built just because Engineers don't understand it or don't like the Designers.

Finally, there is no right way to deliver specifications to Developers. New tools come out every week that automate the creation of specifications, prototypes, and user research findings. The deliverable itself is not important; what's important is that the design and development teams consider that choice together, and that there is a little time for refining deliverables whenever a new process or tool comes into play. Prototypes are often the most useful, and I would expect Designers to spend the most time on them. However, the choice of deliverable should come down to what's best for the Designer and Engineer, full stop.

After the first version is delivered, consider how the team will evolve the design of the existing product. "Technical debt" describes the gradual degradation of code as new features are added or as increased scale must be supported. "**Design debt**" also inevitably accrues if you're doing software right: You try stuff, you learn, some of what you learn has implications for what you've already completed. Debt can occur even within the delivery of a first version, if something designed early in the process needs to be updated later in the product delivery process to account for additions or edits to the design direction. Debt also can accrue naturally over time as the original design becomes unable to handle additional features ("You want to add another tab to the homepage?"). The original UX was designed to create a cohesive experience around a specific set of features. Adding new features breaks that cohesion, reducing consistency and creating a UX that feels increasingly disjointed.

This is another cause of that so-called perfectionism that frustrates Business Leaders. Designers in an environment full of design-debt often sandbag; without support from Business Leaders and Engineering to refactor when it's needed, and worried that they'll never get a chance to come back and "do it right," they'll overestimate timelines and insist on more revisions than anyone else wants. It's true that updating or adding features or updating the visual design takes longer in a disorganized system. And just as Engineers may ask for a complete re-write if too much technical debt builds up, Designers may eventually ask for a complete redesign. Alternatively, someone outside the company, like an investor or board member, might recognize things are a mess. They won't really care how it happened. They're going to ding the product for being unprofessional, dated, or too difficult to use, they're going to call for a redesign, and they're going to be right.

To be clear, this isn't a good thing—like complete rewrites, complete redesigns are risky and time-consuming. Build in headroom for design. Ask your design team what percentage of their time they need to address design debt and they'll love you forever. More importantly, the usability of the user experience will mature over time, rather than degrade. Ask your Designers about reserving 15–20% of their capacity for design debt. This won't insulate you entirely from complete redesigns; in fact, they can be necessary for rebrands or as trends in user experience change. But you will redesign because you want to update, not because your user experience is an embarrassing mess.

Agile, Lean, DevOps, and Other Fancy Words

So far, I've described each step in broad strokes and avoided using specialized words that give a particular spin on the process. However, it's worth outlining today's most popular takes on process, including Agile, Lean, DevOps, and Design Thinking, so you can see how each of them might impact your business.

Agile development eschews uselessly rigorous documentation in favor of regularly delivering working code, created during one- or two-week "sprints." Agile emphasizes flexibility, adjusting as the team learns, and not sticking to a detailed schedule that pretends to predict the unknowns of software development. Dual-track Agile is when Discovery and Design happen alongside or one step ahead of engineering work. Agile is particularly powerful when Product Management, Design, and Engineering employ it together; such a team is well positioned to learn, pivot, and improve quickly.

The **Lean Startup** concept approaches every step as an experiment, identifying what you most need to know, doing the least work you can to learn, and iterating based on what you've learned.

In **DevOps**, you support continuous deployment by mashing up development and operations through technical automation. DevOps is scooping up other disciplines, too, pulling in security and design as part of a "continuous delivery team." "**DesignOps**" or "DesOps" can indicate that a Design team is included in a tightly-coupled Design-Development-Deployment team, but the term most often means the management of design resources, tools, and processes. Some large companies have entire teams dedicated to Design Ops.

Finally, IDEO founder David Kelley's **Design Thinking** is the concept that when given a problem, we first start with deep learning (even empathizing), then generate lots of ideas (not just one), and then test and revise our ideas to come up with a better solution.

All of these, at their heart, are different ways to slice the activities described above, and then integrate teams depending on how the activities are sliced. There is no "right" or perfect way, so select a framework based on principle, not process, and then adjust it based on your team and your goals. As Jeff Gothelf points out, "At the end of the day, your customers don't care whether you practice Agile, Lean, or Design Thinking. They care about great products and services that solve meaningful problems for them in effective ways."

Doing Design in Real-Time

The time devoted to design activities will never be even or sequential. There are many legitimate ways organize the process:

>> **Long Build** (~4 months):
- 5 days Ideating
- 2 days Learning
- 2 weeks Ideating in parallel with Learning
- 3 months Ideating / Refining / Learning / Delivering

>> **Extremely Iterative/ Dual Track Agile** (~2 months):
- 1 day Learning, 1 day Ideating, alternating for 2 weeks
- 1 week Refining
- 1 week Delivering for Sprint 1 in parallel with Ideating / Learning / Refining for Sprint 2, ongoing for 6 weeks

>> **More Complex / Up Front** (~7 months)
- 1 month Modeling and Ideating (in storyboards and prototypes)
- 2 weeks Learning / Refining
- 2 weeks Ideating (in prototypes)
- 1 week Learning / Refining
- 1 month Ideating (in wireframes) in parallel with 1 month Ideating and Refining (in visual design)
- 1 month Refining (in prototypes) in parallel with 1 month Learning
- 3 months Delivering in parallel with Ideating / Learning / Refining

Timeframe, exact steps, and parallel-ness all vary widely depending on the type of company (startup to enterprise), the complexity of the product, how your teams want to work, and degree of risk. Work with your design and engineering teams to figure out what makes the most sense, and assume you'll change your plan a few times as you learn.

FEEDBACK: ASSESSING DESIGN

As a Business Leader, you will be asked for feedback throughout the design process. Don't be worried that you'll need to know something about composition or color schemes. Your design team is depending on you to assess their work and point out risks to meeting business goals—*Is this the best way to take advantage of this opportunity? Has our understanding of the constraints changed?* Focus on providing insight into how the work addresses business risk and opportunity. To this end, there are a few tips for ensuring good feedback sessions.

The Setup

Designers should help everyone involved by recapping how they got to this point (*What did we look at last? What did we say we'd do next?*), and then explaining what you're reviewing today and why. The design team should specify what kind of feedback they are (and are not) looking for, and what the next steps are. As a reviewer, you need to understand exactly what feedback the team wants; request this information at the beginning of any review meeting. Otherwise, you risk focusing your attention in the wrong place—for example, commenting on a particular shade of blue instead of assessing whether the rough mockup helps the user accomplish a complex task. The feedback session should end with a quick recap of what will happen next, to make sure everyone is on the same page. Sometimes, I recap a meeting only to discover that what someone thought was a conclusion was someone else's open question. Recapping at the beginning and the end is crucial for successful feedback sessions; as the Business Leader, it behooves you to make sure this happens.

If you're a Product Manager working daily with the Designers, these "formalities" will occur as quickly as they do in any standup. If you're a CEO or another less involved stakeholder, ensuring good meeting hygiene will exponentially increase the value of the session.

The Feedback

Once the context is set, feedback begins. Business leaders assessing things outside their core expertise may simultaneously feel unsure how to be helpful, anxious to "give good feedback," and compelled to talk. I once watched a stakeholder scroll through a list interface and say that he couldn't find a particular medication—*while tapping the medication he said he couldn't find.* So here are a few things you can do to keep from talking just for the sake of it:

» Focus on intent instead of conventional "feedback." Ask who is using this, why, in what context, and how the designer arrived where they did. A session comprised mostly of questions from stakeholders can be quite productive.

» You bring to this conversation an understanding of the market-opportunity and the technical risks you're taking, the users you're targeting, etc. Ask questions in terms of these risks. "How does engineering feel about this product's feasibility?" Or, "Acme Co., our competitor, has this functionality and people love it. How does ours compare to theirs?"

» It's ok to be quiet for a minute and explore.

» Keep in mind and even state aloud how you are
different from the user. Even if you and the user are
both M.D.s, you think about this product way more
than the they will, and you're using it in a different
context.

» Ask about research sessions, either future ones or
recordings, to understand for yourself how users
react. This also will remind your team to continually
perform user research.

» It's okay for something to look good to you!

Generally, the *type* of feedback you give should align to
where your team is in the process, regardless of what the artifact is.
We can generalize into the same categories I used to describe the
process above:

Learning Feedback

The artifacts produced in the initial learning stage are used to get
the lay of the land (either to understand a particular domain or
to learn from users). Feedback in the form of broad questions is
particularly helpful here. "What is extra? What is missing? What
assumptions are being made?"

Ideating Feedback

In this next phase, you will likely need to wear two hats. Wear the
first when you're helping generate new ideas, or divergent thinking;
and the second when you're helping pare down to the one or two
ideas you'll eventually try, convergent or evaluative thinking. You'll
likely go back and forth between hats (lots of big ideas, then narrow
them down to one; several ways to implement that one big idea,
then narrow down to two of those to test; etc.). Make sure you know
which hat your team needs you to wear, and when.

Because this phase includes artifacts, it's critical for your designer to explain what kind of response they need from you in that moment. You may be helping to generate or evaluate:

» The big idea
» The way a task is accomplished
» The availability of information and functionality on the screen
» The hierarchy of information and functionality on the screen
» The success with which information is communicated
» The success with which the design conveys the brand, personality, or idea

Your design team depends on you to assess what they're presenting based on risks to the business. Does it address the opportunity and fit within constraints?

Ask Design to clarify what feedback they need. You want them to be very clear: "Forget about colors or fonts; do you think this is a good way for the user to accomplish this task?" Even if they're just bouncing an idea off you at a whiteboard, it's still a good idea to ask directly, "Did you want more ideas?" (Should I be generative?) "Or did you want my feedback on this idea?" (Should I be evaluative?)

Getting this part right, and making sure it aligns with the vision (and vice-versa, if an update to the vision is called for) are fundamental to the success of the product.

Refining Feedback

When you're looking at mockups and prototypes, you will be reviewing:

» Screen appearance: colors, fonts, shapes, shading, etc.
» Copy

» Elements: fine-tuning workflows, information, hierarchy, etc.

This is often the biggest chunk of your time giving feedback, but it needn't be onerous. Delegate to and trust your Designers. Don't feel forced to say something just because your team feels obligated to ask.

Most importantly, *stay focused on your intent when you give refining feedback.* Instead of saying, "Can we make that button red?" say, "I'm concerned, users won't see that button—how about you?" And "I want to make sure we're being consistent and following brand guidelines" is more informative than "Is that the right blue?" Saying, "This copy seems really important to me. What do you think about making it more prominent?" is a much more effective way to build collaboration and get the best out of your Designers than, "Make that bold and bump the font size up." At my office, we tell our clients, "We are expensive pencils." If you are the hand and the Designer is just putting on the screen what they're told, you are getting minimal value from them (and they're going to get frustrated). Stating intent and asking questions is an important tactic in engaging their greatest contribution.

The Complexity of the Feedback Process

Designers are not taught to wrangle feedback. Dealing with many opinionated (and at times ill-informed) people is incredibly difficult. You can end up with "design by committee," which erases everything good and interesting and preserves a random mash of the stuff no one criticized. Make sure your designer recognizes the importance of managing feedback well, and give them a chance to explain their thought processes and presentation choices. Simply ask, "How did you come to this design?" Limit the people giving feedback to those who can really contribute something unique and meaningful. Ask (between meetings if appropriate) why each person is there and point out who could be left out of the process. You can pave the way on this front much more easily than a Designer or even a Design Manager can do.

You may also be able to help your design team facing the following challenges:

Asynchronous Feedback

If reviewers are not together when giving feedback, the two (or more) sessions will need to be reconciled. Documenting feedback, ensuring others are on board, and sorting out differences if there isn't agreement can be pretty painful. And if feedback from the two sessions is invisibly "merged," everyone may be unhappy in the subsequent session, sending you back to square one. Help your Designer by avoiding asynchronous feedback sessions whenever possible. Don't look at design work in isolation; unless you're on a very rapid (daily) cycle, reschedule meetings if someone can't make it.

Collecting Feedback from Others

When you're presenting the design team's work to other stakeholders, insist on bringing one Designer along, even just to be a fly on the wall. They may get feedback they'll be expected to respond to, and hearing it directly from the CEO (or Board Member or whomever) is very helpful. It also gives the designer a chance to ask follow-up questions and manage expectations. If the CEO gives unhelpful feedback like, "This button should be red," they can respond directly and immediately about why the button should *not* be red and follow up to understand the CEO's concern better. Using you as the middleman is inefficient.

Feedback and the Org Chart

If the founder, CxO, or the boss says, "This is just an idea; you don't have to do it, I just wondered..." it's going to be difficult for the design team not to implement the idea. Lots of people outrank your Designers—and everyone can easily see what the Designer is doing and weigh in with an opinion. Designers skilled at managing feedback should and will share broadly, but they will do so strategically. If your wild idea really is just that, then make sure the Designer is comfortable deciding to go a different direction, or ask them for several options so they can leverage their expertise.

CHAPTER 4:
CLOSING GOODIES

Here are few tidbits that will help make you a better
Business Leader when it comes to design.

RESEARCH: A HIDDEN RISK

Increasingly, Business Leaders, particularly Product Managers, are getting out there and talking to users. This is GREAT news. If possible, *they should be joined by a researcher or designer* to facilitate shared learning. But some teams don't have anyone experienced in research, or the researcher doesn't have bandwidth for all the demand. (I see this all the time. Good research teams drive demand, demand outstrips their resources, and the teams never "catch up".)

Of course, Product Managers can talk to customers on their own. But we need to consider the garbage-in, garbage-out phenomenon. Product Managers, Founders, and CEOs usually are successful specifically because they're charismatic and persuasive; they're true believers. If they don't change hats when talking to users, then all they'll learn is how persuasive they are. Something as simple as holding a warm drink can impact people's responses to research—so imagine what your brilliantly charismatic personality can do.

When teaching people to do research, I use Beatrice Warde's "Crystal Goblet" analogy. Warde compares typography to a simple crystal wine glass. The purpose of the goblet is to be nearly invisible: to reveal as directly as possible the wine it contains. Similarly, the purpose of typography is to convey the writer's ideas clearly, cleanly, and openly.

You can easily extend this analogy from typography to design, or even technology writ large. But for now, I'd like to use it as a model for how to conduct research.

A researcher's job is to be a crystal goblet. They should be "there" as little as possible, and make space for the research participant to fill. This philosophy grounds all our fundamental rules about facilitating research:

» **Ssssshhhhhh.** Seriously. Just listen. Evaluate yourself by getting a transcript of your research session. Good researchers say a sentence, a few words... and elicit paragraphs of response. They create space for that person to fill.

» **Embrace uncomfortable silence.** Breathe, count to 5, wait. Research participants will be moved to fill the silence with that thing they weren't sure they would share, the thing beyond their pat answer. Listen to what they really have to say.

» **Use incomplete sentences...** This creates an immediate uncomfortable silence and keeps you from introducing bias. Instead of asking, "Would you say this experience was good?" (terrible technique!) or even, "Would you say this experience was good or bad?" (also, not good), allow users to finish your sentence themselves: "Would you say this experience was...?"

» **Use their words.** If you're interviewing someone and they say "wirey thing-y," don't say "dongle"; say "wirey thing-y." Remember, you're trying to be there as little as possible. Using their words means you're not asserting your presence and not implicitly offering correction.

» **Don't ask them to be crystal balls.** Data show that people stink at predicting their future actions, and attitude is a terrible predictor of behavior. A user telling you they'll buy your product in the future has almost nothing to do with whether or not they actually will. You can, however, *ask* them to buy it, and check later to see if they actually did. If you must ask for predictions, it's better to ask what your research participants think other people like them would do.

» **Be invisible after research.** When you're considering what you've learned, be careful not to insert your own ideas. Confirmation bias is impossible to avoid entirely. But being aware of your biases, even explicitly listing them, can help you limit them. It also helps to consult with other people who don't care as much about the outcome.

HOW TO BE YOUR TEAM'S FAVORITE BOSS / CLIENT / COLLABORATOR

Your team will love working for you if:

» You value design as a strategic differentiator, and that's built into your product vision. You are 100% confident that design will make your business more successful.

» You expect Designers to go much deeper than colors and fonts. You invite them to be involved from the very beginning of the process: conducting research, creating models, collaborating with Engineering on what's technically feasible, designing workflows, and developing systems.

» You expect Designers to be ultimately responsible for the Design of your entire product.

» You expect Designers to work closely with Product Management and Engineering, and vice-versa.

» You collaborate on how requirements are developed and delivered.

» You might start a conversation talking about screens, but what you really want to discuss is intent (no napkins, no treating Designers as pencils).

» You ask lots of questions during feedback sessions.

» You understand that Product Design and Marketing are different skills that are almost always best handled by different teams.

» You ask what your Design team needs from you.

» You don't think of yourself as the perfect token user.

» You are an expert in the market and subject matter, and you are happy to share what you know.

» You are interested in what you can learn from your Design team.

» You are interested in what you can learn from users.

» You minimize the number of reviewers, but protect the review process.

» You understand the relative importance of various decisions, and you value your own expertise as well as others'.

» You don't get stuck in derivative thinking (just refining old ideas); you welcome big new ideas when they're appropriate.

» You trust in Design and the Design Process.

» You have lots of ideas, but don't value them above others. Your ego is separated from your ideas, and you value your team's input and feedback.

» You help the team get the resources (data, budget, user access, etc.) they need to do their jobs well.

TOMORROW'S TO-DOS

I'll wrap up with five suggestions for things to do differently tomorrow based on what you've learned here.

1. **Partner with your design team to score your maturity and set a new goal.** Score your organization based on one of the indices in Chapter 1.

2. **Figure out your ratio of Designers to Engineers.** Begin to sort out what it should be, using the method in Chapter 2.

3. If you don't have a design team (or it's small), **call three design consultancies** just to chat about how they might help. See what you learn from those conversations.

4. If you have Designers, **schedule or go to a feedback meeting.** Ask the questions described in Chapter 3:
   » Where are we in the process? What happened last? What happens next?
   » Who is in the room? Why?
   » Is anyone else reviewing this? When? How is their feedback integrated with ours?
   » What feedback and input do you need today?
   » Ask 5 intent-related questions by way of giving feedback.

5. **Put research on your calendar.** Sit in on the research sessions! Ask the moderator about their philosophy or perspective on moderation.

READING LIST

This book barely scratches the surface of design. I've provided a list of online articles and reasonably-sized books if you want to learn more, and your Designers will be a great source of recommendations as well.

On the Value of Design

The Total Economic Impact™ Of IBM's Design Thinking Practice,
Forrester, download PDF online.
https://www.ibm.com/design/thinking/static/media/Enterprise-
Design-Thinking-Report.8ab1e9e1.pdf

The Business Value of Design, McKinsey, download PDF online.
https://www.mckinsey.com/business-functions/
mckinsey-design/our-insights/the-business-value-of-design

Designing a Future Economy, UK Design Council, download PDF
online. https://www.designcouncil.org.uk/what-we-do/research/
designing-future-economy

*Design Index: The Impact of Design on Stock Market
Performance,* online article by UK Design Council. https://
designbusinesscouncil.com/wp-content/uploads/2017/08/
design_index_9199.pdf

Design Value Index: Results and Commentary, Design Management
Institute, download PDF online. https://www.dmi.org/page/
DesignValue/The-Value-of-Design-.htm

Factfinder: The Value of Design, UK Design Council, download
PDF online. https://www.designcouncil.org.uk/resources/report/
factfinder-value-design

*IDEO Studied Innovation in 100+ Companies—Here's What It
Found,* Fast Company web page.
https://www.fastcompany.com/3069069/ideo-studied-innovation-
in-100-companies-heres-what-it-found

Measuring Design and its Role in Innovation, Organization for Economic Co-operation and Development (OECD), web page. http://www.oecd.org/science/inno/measuring-design-and-innovation.htm

The Future of Design in Startups, NEA, download PDF online. http://www.futureof.design/

Foundational Design Books and Articles

The Elements of User Experience: User-Centered Design for the Web and Beyond, book by Jesse James Garrett, New Riders; 2 edition (December 26, 2010). https://www.amazon.com/Elements-User-Experience-User-Centered-Design/dp/0321683684

The Design of Everyday Things, book by Don Norman, Basic Books; Revised, Expanded edition (November 5, 2013). https://www.amazon.com/Design-Everyday-Things-Revised-Expanded/dp/0465050654/

The Inmates are Running the Asylum: Why High Tech Products Drive Us Crazy and How to Restore the Sanity, book by Alan Cooper, Sams - Pearson Education; 1 edition (March 5, 2004). https://www.amazon.com/Inmates-Are-Running-Asylum-Products/dp/0672326140/

Alan Cooper and the Goal-Directed Design Process, online article by Hugh Dubberly. http://www.dubberly.com/articles/alan-cooper-and-the-goal-directed-design-process.html

Don't Make Me Think: A Common Sense Approach to Web Usability book by Steve Krug. https://www.amazon.com/Dont-Make-Think-Revisited-Usability/dp/0321965515/

Design Principles and Feedback

Design principles to choose the right ideas, web site by Henk Wijnholds

Principles.design, web site by Ben Brignell

designprinciplesftw.com, web site by Meetod

Discussing Design: Improving Communication and Collaboration through Critique, book by Adam Connor and Aaron Irizarry

On Vision and Process

Inspired: How the Best Companies Create Technology-Powered Products and Services, book by Marty Cagan, Wiley; 2 edition (December 4, 2017). https://svpg.com/inspired-how-to-create-products-customers-love/

Outcomes Over Output, book by Josh Seiden, Sense and Respond Press (April 8, 2019). https://www.senseandrespondpress.com/managing-outcomes

Making Progress: The 7 Responsibilities of the Innovation Leader, book by Ryan Jacoby, Sense and Respond Press (December 13, 2017). https://www.senseandrespondpress.com/making-progress

Lean vs. Agile vs. Design Thinking, book by Jeff Gothelf, Sense and Respond Press (October 6, 2017). https://www.senseandrespondpress.com/lean-vs-agile-vs-design-thinking

Manifesto for Agile Software Development, web page by various authors. https://agilemanifesto.org/

Continuous Discovery, online article by Marty Cagan. https://svpg.com/continuous-discovery/

Process vs. Model (on dual track agile), online article by Marty Cagan. https://svpg.com/process-vs-model/

Dual Track Development is not Duel Track (on dual track agile), online article by Jeff Patton. https://www.jpattonassociates.com/dual-track-development/

Finding the Speed to Innovate (on DevOps), online article by McKinsey. https://www.mckinsey.com/business-functions/mckinsey-digital/our-insights/finding-the-speed-to-innovate

What is design operations and why should you care? (on DesignOps), online article by Dave Malouf. https://medium.com/designer-hangout/what-is-design-operations-and-why-should-you-care-b72f02b47761

On Hiring and Salaries

Creative & Marketing Salary Guide, by Robert Half, downline PDF online. https://www.roberthalf.com/salary-guide

Design Salary Survey, O'Reilly, downline PDF online.
https://www.oreilly.com/design/free/files/2017-design-salary-survey.pdf (or search for the latest)

Org Design for Design Orgs: Building and Managing In-House Design Teams, book by Kristin Skinner and Peter Merholz, O'Reilly Media; 1 edition (September 3, 2016).
https://orgdesignfordesignorgs.com/

On Research

Experiencing Physical Warmth Promotes Interpersonal Warmth (on warm cups of coffee), by Lawrence E. Williams and John A. Bargh, download PDF online. https://www.ncbi.nlm.nih.gov/pmc/articles/PMC2737341/

Being the Crystal Goblet (the essay and more on this idea), online article by Audrey Crane. https://medium.com/@DesignMap.com/being-the-crystal-goblet-706b6c3522a

User research interviews: An interview with Steve Portigal (the Tivo story), online article by Steve Portigal and Gerry Gaffney.
https://uxpod.com/user-research-interviews-an-interview-with-steve-portigal/

Attitudes and Behavior (on what poor predictors attitudes are), online article by Saul McLeod. https://www.simplypsychology.org/attitudes.html

Miscellaneous

To Spec or Not to Spec? What a Stupid Question, online article by Upwork. https://www.upwork.com/blog/2010/02/to-spec-or-not-to-spec-what-a-stupid-question/

Spec | #saynotospec, YouTube video by Zulu Alpha Kilo. https://www.youtube.com/watch?v=8y5IaCQA86o

ACKNOWLEDGMENTS

This book is essentially a massive collaboration over the years of mentors, clients, and my colleagues and Partners at DesignMap. I've had the great good fortune to learn from so many talented, open-minded and open-hearted people, and I am grateful to all of you. In particular, many core ideas put forth here were born from countless conversations with my colleagues Jason Frasier and Rob Gardziel, one on each shoulder! My Partners at DesignMap, Nathan Kendrick, Greg Baker, and Chuck Moore, gave me encouragement and understanding for much longer than any of us expected when I first got excited about writing this book. The eternal patience and support of Josh, Jeff and Vicky gave this book polish and sensibility and kept me from losing heart when trying to tackle such a massive subject. I was astonishingly lucky to have the generosity of friends who were willing to take the time out of their busy lives to contribute substantially to the content and my confidence: Marty Cagan, Jeff Patton, Andy Cerio, and Scott Johnston. Of course, nothing would have happened without Kyle Porter, who sparked the idea for this book, and my mother and father, who gave me the chance to be excited about tech when that meant cutting up punchcards to make paper dolls!

Finally, I'm deeply grateful for the patience of my long-suffering, brilliant and resourceful daughters, Clementine, Calliope and Autumn, while I was stretched thin trying to make this happen (plus every other crazy scheme their mom gets excited about). And to my fiancé Terry, thank you for the eternal reading, re-reading, conversation and perspective—thank you for being my editor, my partner, and for helping finally put it all together.

Unless you count that computer program Audrey wrote on a TRS-80 when she was 5, **AUDREY CRANE**'s tech career really got started at Netscape, where she had the extraordinary good luck to meet two of the most important mentors in her life, Hugh Dubberly and Marty Cagan. Since then, she's worked both inside companies and externally as a consultant. She loves figuring out how to make good business by making people's lives better at places like Docker, Salesforce, and eBay.

Audrey is a Partner at DesignMap, a strategic product design agency, that helps ambitious enterprise software companies and startups make inflection points happen through UX strategy, discovery, design, and building core UX competency.

Audrey is excited to be engaged (finally!) to her high school sweetheart and very patient editor. She is Mom to three amazing daughters, Clementine, Calliope, and Autumn, and Stepmom-to-be to Forest, Victoria, Rain, Samantha and Shiloh.

www.designmap.com
🐦 **@audcrane**
📷 **@audcrane**
💼 **audcrane**

Made in the USA
Coppell, TX
29 February 2020